MILKSHAKE BAR

SHAKES, MALTS, FLOATS & OTHER
SODA FOUNTAIN CLASSICS

MILKSHAKE BAR

SHAKES, MALTS, FLOATS & OTHER SODA FOUNTAIN CLASSICS

HANNAH MILES

PHOTOGRAPHY BY KATE WHITAKER

RYLAND
PETERS
& SMALL

LONDON NEW YORK

DEDICATION
For Sacha, who makes the best mango lassi.

SENIOR DESIGNER Megan Smith
EDITOR Rebecca Woods
HEAD OF PRODUCTION Patricia Harrington
ART DIRECTOR Leslie Harrington
EDITORIAL DIRECTOR Julia Charles

PROP STYLIST Liz Belton
FOOD STYLIST Sunil Vijayakar
INDEXER Hilary Bird

First published in 2012
by Ryland Peters & Small
20–21 Jockey's Fields,
London WC1R 4BW
and
519 Broadway, 5th Floor,
New York NY 10012

www.rylandpeters.com

10 9 8 7 6 5 4 3 2 1

Text © Hannah Miles 2012
Design and photographs
© Ryland Peters & Small 2012

ISBN: 978-1-84975-191-9

Printed and bound in China

A CIP record for this book is available from the British Library.

US Library of Congress Cataloging-in-Publication Data has been applied for.

AUTHOR'S ACKNOWLEDGEMENTS
With thanks to RPS for allowing me to indulge my milkshake dreams, particularly Rebecca for the patient editing, Julia for the pistachio milkshake inspiration and Megan for the beautiful book design. With every thanks to Sunil for making such beautiful milkshakes, to Liz for the perfect props and to Kate for the stunning photography. Love and hugs to my brother Gareth for the US Crunchie bar research! To all my lovely milkshake tasters – you know who you are - thanks for slurping all that milkshake!

CONTENTS

SHAKE IT UP!

Tasting my first milkshake is a memory that sticks clearly in my mind. Sitting on a red leather banquette in Ed's Easy Diner in London, I enjoyed my first chocolate and peanut butter milkshake. I was hooked at the first sip. Who doesn't delight in an ice cold glass of milk or a thick milkshake supped through a straw? These recipes will transport you to your favourite milkshake bar or soda fountain – there are classic coke floats and strawberry shakes, as well as new treats like the honeycomb shake or doughnut float.

The main requirement of a good milkshake is a bubbly foamy top. In this field, fizzy floats come into their own – as soon as you pour soda over ice cream it froths in an almost magical way. All are easy to make at home – a blender, soda glasses and straws are the only equipment needed and most ingredients are easily available. I always have a tub of vanilla ice cream in the freezer so when the call for a milkshake comes, I am prepared.

This book contains not only milkshakes but also other delicious creamy drinks such as the Mango Lassi or Berry Smoothie, as well as more refreshing drinks like the Apple Snow Shake or Mint and Pineapple Crush. For low-fat versions of these drinks, you can use skimmed milk, low-fat ice cream (or frozen yogurt) and sugar-free fizzy drinks. For super-cold drinks, chill your glasses in the freezer before using.

All drinks in this book are made to fill 300 ml/ 10 oz. glasses and serve two, but you can easily halve the ingredients to make a drink for one or double the ingredients if you are serving more people. My brother even went as far as to set up a milkshake bar at a friend's wedding as his gift to them. He made over 200 milkshakes in one afternoon, which must be a record! Whatever flavours tickle your taste buds, there is guaranteed to be a milkshake in this book to suit you. All aboard the milkshake float!

The recipes below are for basic syrups and sauces that are used in the recipes in this book. They are perfect in milkshakes or simply drizzled over ice cream.

BASIC RECIPES

BERRY SAUCE

200 g/6½ oz. strawberries, hulled
150 g/5 oz. raspberries
150 g/¾ cup caster/granulated
    sugar
1 teaspoon vanilla extract

MAKES 250 ML/1 CUP

Put all the ingredients in a small saucepan set over low heat and simmer until the sugar has dissolved, the fruit is very soft and the sauce is syrupy.

Pass the sauce through a sieve/ strainer, pressing the juice from the fruit using the back of a spoon. Once cooled, pour into a bottle.

This sauce will store in the fridge in a sealed bottle for up to 1 week.

CHOCOLATE SYRUP

125 g/⅔ cup packed dark
    brown sugar
125 g/⅔ cup caster/granulated
    sugar
70 g/½ cup unsweetened
    cocoa powder, sifted
1 teaspoon vanilla extract
a pinch of salt

MAKES 500 ML/2 CUPS

Put all the ingredients and 250 ml/ 1 cup water in a small saucepan set over low heat. Simmer until the sugar has dissolved, then increase the heat to medium and simmer, stirring, until the sauce is thick and syrupy.

Once cooled, the syrup will store in the fridge in a sealed bottle for up to 3 weeks.

CARAMEL SAUCE

100 g/½ cup caster/granulated
    sugar
50 g/3 tablespoons butter
100 ml/6 tablespoons double/
    heavy cream
a pinch of salt

MAKES 200 ML/¾ CUP

Put the sugar and butter in a small saucepan set over low heat and simmer gently, stirring, until the sugar and butter have dissolved. Add the salt and stir again. Add cream and heat until the sauce is thick and a golden caramel colour. If the sauce becomes too thick, add a little further cream.

Once cooled, this sauce will store in the fridge in a sealed jar for up to 1 week.

CLASSICS

There are various claims to the creation of the first ice cream float, the most popular being that a soda seller ran out of ice to chill his sodas and added ice cream to keep his drinks cool. While these may be the simplest of drinks to prepare, I have never known one more easily able to put a smile on people's faces. You can use any combination of fizzy drink and ice cream (or sorbet) of your choice – half the fun is coming up with new creations. The soda foam disappears quickly so you need to serve these drinks immediately – or why not let your guests pour over the soda themselves?

FLOATS

COKE FLOAT

4 scoops vanilla ice cream
1 teaspoon vanilla extract
500 ml/2 cups cola, chilled

2 soda glasses, chilled

SERVES 2

Put one scoop of ice cream and ½ teaspoon vanilla extract in the bottom of each glass. Fill each glass with cola and top with a second scoop of ice cream. Serve immediately.

CREAM SODA FLOAT

4 scoops lemon sorbet
500 ml/2 cups cream soda, chilled

2 soda glasses, chilled

SERVES 2

Put one scoop of sorbet in the bottom of each glass. Fill each glass with cream soda and top with a second scoop of sorbet. Serve immediately.

11

Of all the milkshakes in this book that my recipe tasters tested, this one came out on top. I was even asked to make seconds! Rich caramel banana milk – this drink is a must for banana lovers. If you are not able to find banana ice cream, you can substitute vanilla ice cream for equally delicious results.

BANANA CARAMEL MILKSHAKE

4 tablespoons Caramel Sauce
   (see page 8 or store-bought),
   plus extra to drizzle
2 ripe bananas, peeled and sliced
500 ml/2 cups milk, chilled
4 scoops banana or vanilla
   ice cream
a few drops of yellow food
   colouring (optional)
2 dried banana chips, to decorate

2 soda glasses, chilled
2 straws

SERVES 2

Spoon 1 tablespoon of the caramel sauce into each glass and swirl the glass until there is a thin coating of caramel sauce over the bottom half of the glass. This will give a pretty two tone effect when the milkshake is poured in.

Put the bananas in a blender with the milk, 2 tablespoons caramel sauce, two scoops of the ice cream and the food colouring, if using, and whizz until very foamy and thick.

Pour the milkshake into chilled glasses and top with a second scoop of ice cream. Decorate each glass with a dried banana chip and a drizzle of caramel sauce and serve immediately with straws.

These milkshakes are inspired by the popular children's Mini Milk ice lollies – simply flavoured with vanilla, strawberry and chocolate. No fuss, no frills, just delicious flavoured milk. They are served in mini milk bottles for a super cute effect, so the servings are smaller than the other drinks, but simply scale up the recipe if you are very thirsty.

MINI MILK SHAKES

VANILLA

½ vanilla pod/bean
60 g/⅓ cup caster/granulated
    sugar
200 ml/¾ cup milk, chilled

SERVES 2

To make the vanilla syrup, cut the vanilla pod in half lengthways and scoop out the vanilla seeds using a teaspoon. Put the pod and seeds in a small saucepan with the sugar and 80 ml/⅓ cup water and simmer gently for about 10 minutes until you have a thin syrup. Remove from the heat and allow to cool completely, then remove the vanilla pod.

Add 2 tablespoons of the cooled vanilla syrup to the milk and whisk together using a small whisk or fork. Pour into 2 mini milk bottles and serve with straws.

STRAWBERRY

200 ml/¾ cup milk, chilled
1 tablespoon Berry Sauce
    (see page 8) or store-bought
    strawberry sauce
4 large ripe strawberries
1 tablespoon vanilla syrup (see
    recipe, left) or 1 teaspoon
    vanilla extract and 1 tablespoon
    caster/granulated sugar

SERVES 2

Pour the milk into a blender and add the berry sauce, strawberries and vanilla syrup. Blitz for a few seconds until light and frothy.

Pass the milkshake through a sieve/strainer to strain out the strawberry seeds and then pour into 2 mini milk bottles and serve with straws.

CHOCOLATE

2 tablespoons Chocolate Syrup
    (see page 8 or store-bought)
200 ml/¾ cup milk, chilled

SERVES 2

In a jug/pitcher, whisk the chocolate syrup into the milk. Pour into two mini milk bottles and serve with straws.

With Reese's peanut butter chocolates my all time favourite candy, you can imagine how much I like this milkshake. Rich chocolate syrup, salty peanut butter and a drizzle of caramel, all served ice cold with ice cream – quite simply heaven in a glass for me! You can use smooth or crunchy peanut butter, whichever you prefer. If you use crunchy, you may want to serve your milkshakes with a spoon so that you can eat the peanut pieces, which will sink to the bottom of the shake.

PEANUT BUTTER SHAKE

2 tablespoons Chocolate Syrup
(see page 8 or store-bought)
4 tablespoons Caramel Sauce
(see page 8 or store-bought)
500 ml/2 cups milk, chilled
100 g/½ cup peanut butter
4 scoops vanilla ice cream
10 g/1 tablespoon honey roasted
peanuts, chopped, to decorate

2 soda glasses, chilled
a squeezy bottle (optional)
2 straws

SERVES 2

Drizzle alternating lines of chocolate syrup and caramel sauce down the inside of each glass using a squeezy bottle or a spoon (use about 1 tablespoon of each sauce per glass).

Add the remaining two tablespoons of caramel sauce to a blender with the milk, peanut butter and two scoops of ice cream and whizz until very foamy and thick.

Pour the milkshake into the prepared glasses, top each with a scoop of ice cream and sprinkle with the peanuts. Serve immediately with straws.

Rest assured those of you who are not familiar with this soda fountain classic, 'Egg cream' no longer contains eggs or cream! This is a chocolate soda drink with a creamy foam top and is very refreshing – a lighter version of a chocolate milkshake. It has a place close to my heart as it is said to originate from Brooklyn, where my brother Gareth lives.

EGG CREAM

2 tablespoons Chocolate Syrup
   (see page 8 or store-bought)
250 ml/1 cup milk, chilled
250 ml/1 cup soda water, chilled

2 soda glasses, chilled

SERVES 2

In a jug/pitcher whisk together the chocolate syrup and the milk until all the syrup is dissolved.

Pour the chocolate milk into chilled glasses and top up with the soda. The drinks will foam immediately so you need to serve them straight away.

Chocolate malt shakes are one of my favourites. There is something very comforting about the flavour of malt – it reminds me of the warm, malted drinks that we were given at bedtime as children. This one is topped with malted chocolates and served with chocolate ice cream, yum yum!

CHOCOLATE MALT SHAKE

4 tablespoons Chocolate Syrup
   (see page 8, or store-bought)
500 ml/2 cups milk, chilled
30 g/1 oz. malted milk powder
   (such as Horlicks)
4 scoops chocolate ice cream
10 milk chocolate-coated malted
   milk balls (such as Maltesers),
   to decorate

2 soda glasses, chilled
a squeezy bottle or piping bag
   with a small round nozzle/tip

SERVES 2

Put two tablespoons of the chocolate syrup in a squeezy bottle or piping bag and drizzle pretty patterns of syrup up the inside of each glass.

Put the milk in a blender with the malted milk powder, 2 scoops of the ice cream and the remaining chocolate syrup. Whizz until very foamy and thick.

Cut the malted milk balls in half using a sharp knife. Pour the milkshake into the prepared glasses, top each with a scoop of chocolate ice cream and decorate with the malted milk balls. Serve immediately.

This vanilla milkshake may be simple but it is utterly delicious and perfectly refreshing on a hot summer's day. For a vanilla chocolate malt, just add two tablespoons of chocolate syrup to the blender with the other ingredients.

VANILLA MALT FRAPPE

½ **vanilla pod/bean**
400 ml/1⅔ **cup milk, chilled**
60 g/6 **tablespoons malted milk powder (such as Horlicks)**
4 **scoops vanilla ice cream**
10–15 **ice cubes**

2 *soda glasses, chilled*
2 *straws*

SERVES 2

Cut the vanilla pod in half lengthways and scoop out the vanilla seeds using a teaspoon. Put the seeds in a blender with the milk, malt powder, ice cream and ice cubes and whizz until thick and foamy and the ice has been crushed. If your blender is not strong enough to crush ice, place the ice cubes in a plastic bag, seal and wrap in a clean dish towel, and bash the bag with a wooden rolling pin until the ice is crushed. Then add to the blender and blitz.

Pour the milkshake into chilled glasses and serve immediately with straws.

TIP Don't throw away the discarded vanilla pod as it still has a delicious flavour. Wash and dry the pod then pack in a Kilner jar filled with sugar. Leave for 3 weeks for delicately scented vanilla sugar, perfect for baking cakes and cookies.

FRUITY

Apple snow is a creamy apple mousse dessert made with whipped cream and apple purée. It is best made with whipped egg white for lightness, but this can be omitted if you are serving the shake to people who cannot eat raw egg.

APPLE SNOW SHAKE

FOR THE APPLE SNOW

2 green apples, peeled, cored
   and thinly sliced
freshly squeezed juice of
   ½ lemon
30 g/2½ tablespoons caster/
   granulated sugar
150 ml/⅔ cup double/heavy
   cream
1 egg white

FOR THE APPLE SLUSHIE

200 ml/¾ cup cloudy apple juice
10 ice cubes

green sugar sprinkles,
   to decorate
apple slices, to decorate

*2 sundae or large martini
   glasses, chilled*

SERVES 2

Put the apple slices in a heavy-based saucepan with the lemon juice, sugar and 3 tablespoons water, and simmer until the apple is very soft. Leave to cool, then purée using a stick blender.

In a large mixing bowl, whip the cream to stiff peaks. In a separate bowl, whip the egg white to stiff peaks. Fold the egg white and apple purée into the whipped cream and store in the fridge until needed.

For the apple slushie, put the apple juice and ice cubes in a blender and whizz until the ice is crushed. If your blender is not strong enough to crush ice, place the ice cubes in a plastic bag, seal and wrap in a clean dish towel, and bash the bag with a rolling pin until the ice is crushed. Then add to the blender with the apple juice and blend.

Pour the apple slushie into chilled glasses and top with a spoonful of the apple snow. Decorate with sprinkles and apple slices and serve immediately.

Lemon meringue pie is one of my favourite desserts: the combination of light caramelized meringue and tangy lemon cream is just delicious! This is my milkshake version: a lemon yogurt drink, topped with a crisp delicate meringue. Serve with a spoon so that you can eat the meringue when you have finished the drink.

LEMON MERINGUE

3 tablespoons lemon curd
300 ml/1¼ cups lemon yogurt
3 scoops lemon or vanilla
   ice cream
300 ml/1¼ cups milk, chilled
2 mini meringues

2 soda glasses, chilled
2 straws
a squeezy bottle or piping bag
   with a small round nozzle/tip

SERVES 2

Put two tablespoons of the lemon curd in a squeezy bottle or piping bag and pipe a lemon spiral onto the inside of each glass.

Put the yogurt, ice cream, milk and remaining tablespoon of lemon curd in a blender and whizz until smooth.

Pour into the prepared glasses and top each with a meringue. Serve immediately with straws and a spoon to eat the meringue.

Smoothies are popular yogurt-based drinks that are really refreshing. Made with frozen berries, which defrost as you blend, this drink has the perfect chill factor. You can use any combination of berries you like – strawberries, blueberries and raspberries are my favourites. Decorated with fresh fruit skewers, this cooling drink is perfect to serve when the sun shines.

BERRY SMOOTHIE

8–10 fresh berries of your choice (strawberries, blackberries and raspberries work well)

2 tablespoons Berry Sauce (see page 8) or store-bought strawberry sauce

300 ml/1¼ cups natural yogurt

300 ml/1¼ cups milk, chilled

150 g/1 cup fresh ripe strawberries

250 g/2 cups frozen summer berries

1 teaspoon vanilla extract

1 tablespoon runny honey, or to taste

2 wooden skewers

a squeezy bottle or piping bag with a small round nozzle/tip

2 soda glasses, chilled

2 straws

SERVES 2

Thread several berries onto each of the skewers and store in the fridge until needed.

Put two tablespoons of the berry sauce in a squeezy bottle or piping bag and pipe a spiral onto the inside of each glass.

Put the yogurt and milk in a blender, add the strawberries, frozen berries, vanilla extract and honey and blitz until all the fruit is blended. If your blender is not strong enough to crush the frozen berries, allow them to soften at room temperature before adding.

Pass the smoothie through a sieve/strainer to remove the seeds, then pour into the prepared glasses. Add a fruit skewer and straw to each glass and serve.

TIP The sweetness may need to be adjusted depending on the sugar content of the berries. Add a little more honey if necessary.

My husband Sacha is Indian and lassis (Indian milk drinks) are very popular in our household, especially mango flavour. Although you can use fresh mango, we prefer the flavour that tinned mango purée gives and it is certainly less work. This is Sacha's recipe – although it may seem strange to add salt and cumin to a sweet drink, they really bring out the flavour of the mango. For best results use runny yogurt rather than set and the brightest green pistachios you can find.

MANGO LASSI

¼ teaspoon cumin seeds

¼ teaspoon sea salt

360 ml/1½ cups golden mango purée

300 m/1¼ cups plain yogurt, plus 2 teaspoons to serve

200 ml/¾ cup milk, chilled

1 tablespoon shelled pistachios, finely chopped, to decorate

edible gold leaf, to decorate (optional)

2 tall glasses, chilled

SERVES 2

Crush the cumin seeds and salt to a fine powder in a mortar and pestle.

Spoon 2 tablespoons of the mango purée into each glass and swirl so that the bottom half of the glass is covered with a thick layer of purée. This will give a pretty two tone effect when you fill the glass.

Put the yogurt, milk and the rest of the mango purée in a blender with the crushed cumin and salt and blitz until smooth.

Pour into the prepared glasses and add a teaspoon of yogurt to the top of each. Sprinkle with the chopped pistachios and a few flakes of gold leaf, if using, and serve immediately.

On a hot day, chilled slices of watermelon are a welcome respite from the heat. To make the drink a little more grown up, add a shot of tequila or white rum.

WATERMELON COOLER

1 small ripe seedless watermelon
  (about 800 g/1¾ lbs. flesh
  is needed)
freshly squeezed juice of 3 limes
20 ice cubes
sugar, to taste
lime wedges, to serve (optional)

melon baller
2 wooden skewers
2 soda glasses, chilled
2 straws

SERVES 2

Using the melon baller, make 6 balls of melon and thread 3 onto each skewer. Cover the skewers and store in the fridge until needed.

Chop the remaining watermelon flesh and squeeze the juice from the remaining limes (removing any pips). Put the lime juice and watermelon flesh in a blender with the ice cubes and blitz to a smooth purée. If your blender is not strong enough to crush ice, place the ice cubes in a plastic bag, seal and wrap in a clean dish towel, and bash the bag with a wooden rolling pin until the ice is crushed. Then add to the blender and blitz with the watermelon.

Taste the drink for sweetness. If it is too sour, add a little sugar and blend again.

Pour into chilled glasses and serve with straws, melon swizzle sticks and wedges of lime, if using.

I was given the recipe for this drink at the lovely Layana Hotel in Thailand – a tropical paradise where the days drift by in a haze of sunshine. It is so refreshing with a citrus tang from the lemon and a heady scent of mint.

MINT AND PINEAPPLE CRUSH

1 green apple, cored and chopped
1 lemon, cut into 8 wedges and pips removed
2 tablespoons chopped fresh mint
2 teaspoons caster/granulated sugar
300 ml/1¼ cups pineapple juice
300 ml/1¼ cups mango juice
12 ice cubes
pineapple wedges, to decorate
fresh mint sprigs, to decorate

muddler or rolling pin
cocktail shaker
2 tall glasses, chilled

SERVES 2

Put the apple and lemon pieces in a jug/pitcher, add the mint and sugar, and pound together with a muddler or the end of a rolling pin.

Tip the muddled fruit into a cocktail shaker and add the pineapple and mango juices and a few ice cubes. Shake vigorously to mix and chill the drink.

Strain into ice-filled, chilled glasses and serve with a small wedge of pineapple and a mint sprig garnishing each glass.

This creamy smoothie, flavoured with banana and coconut, is a real treat. Served in a fun coconut- and chocolate-rimmed glass, it is the perfect party drink. Coconut yogurt is available in most supermarkets, but if you can't find it replace with plain yogurt and two tablespoons of coconut cream.

BANANA AND COCONUT SMOOTHIE

2 ripe bananas, peeled and sliced
400 g/1¾ cups coconut yogurt
300 ml/1¼ cups milk, chilled
2 tablespoons maple syrup
a few drops of yellow food
   colouring (optional)

FOR THE GLASSES
30 g/1 oz. plain/dark chocolate
20 g/3 tablespoons dessicated/
   dried shredded coconut

2 soda glasses
2 straws

SERVES 2

To prepare the glasses, melt the chocolate in a heatproof bowl set over a saucepan of simmering water. Don't to let the water touch the bottom of the bowl. When melted, carefully remove the bowl from the pan.

Toast the coconut in a dry frying pan, stirring all the time, until it starts to turn golden brown. Tip onto a plate. Dip the rim of each glass in the melted chocolate, then press into the toasted coconut. Set aside until you are ready to serve.

Put the bananas in a blender with the yogurt, milk, maple syrup and a few drops of yellow food colouring, if using, and blitz until smooth and frothy. Taste for sweetness, adding a little more maple syrup if needed.

Pour into the prepared glasses and serve immediately with straws.

FUN

Chocolate-covered honeycomb bubbles, which have a brittle crunch when you bite, are the centrepiece of this delicious caramel flavoured milkshake. If you can't find honeycomb ice cream, look out for honeycomb choc ices (such as the Crunchie bar choc ice) or substitute vanilla ice cream and add a little extra honeycomb to the milkshake.

HONEYCOMB SHAKE

4 scoops honeycomb or vanilla
   ice cream
500 ml/2 cups milk
40 g/1½ oz. chocolate-covered
   honeycomb/sponge candy,
   roughly chopped

2 soda glasses, chilled
2 straws

SERVES 2

Put two scoops of the ice cream in a blender with the milk and ¾ of the chocolate-covered honeycomb, and blitz until thick and creamy.

Pour the milkshake into the chilled glasses, top each glass with a second scoop of ice cream and sprinkle with the remaining chopped honeycomb. Serve immediately with straws.

Milk and cookies – the perfect after-school treat – are made extra special in this recipe. As the ice cubes melt, the chocolate syrup turns the milk chocolatey. It might seem a little unusual to add crisps and pretzels to a cookie, but the saltiness and white chocolate work perfectly together.

ICED MILK AND COOKIES

FOR THE CHOCOLATE ICE CUBES
330 ml/1⅓ cups water
2 tablespoons Chocolate Syrup
  (see page 8 or store-bought)

FOR THE PRETZEL COOKIES
125 g/1 stick butter, softened
120 g/½ cup caster/granulated
  sugar
200 g/1⅔ cups plain/all-purpose
  flour, sifted
1 teaspoon baking powder
1 large egg
1 teaspoon vanilla extract
60 g/2 oz. pretzels
30 g/1 oz. ready salted
  crisps/potato chips
200 g/1⅓ cups white chocolate
  chips

ice-cold milk, to serve

*two baking sheets, greased
  and lined*
2 silicon ice cube trays
2 tall glasses

SERVES 2, MAKES 16 COOKIES

For the chocolate ice cubes, whisk together the water and chocolate syrup and pour into ice cube trays. Freeze overnight in the freezer.

Preheat the oven to 180°C (350°F) Gas 4.

Put the butter and sugar in a large mixing bowl and beat with an electric whisk until pale and creamy. Add the flour, baking powder, egg and vanilla extract and whisk again to form a soft dough. Add the pretzels, crisps and white chocolate and whisk again so that everything is incorporated. The pretzels and crisps may break up as you mix.

Place tablespoonfuls of the cookie mixture onto the prepared baking sheets, a small distance apart as they will spread a little during cooking, and bake for 10–15 minutes until golden brown on top but still slightly soft in the middle. Allow to cool on the sheets for a few minutes then transfer to a wire rack to cool completely.

Fill tall glasses with chocolate ice cubes and top up with chilled milk. Serve with the cookies on the side. Any leftover cookies can be stored in an airtight container for up to 5 days.

This jammy float is a real treat, served with mini doughnut skewers on the side. You can either buy packs of mini doughnuts in a supermarket, or even make your own homemade ones, which are wonderful served warm with the cool shake.

DOUGHNUT FLOAT

4 tablespoons strawberry
   jam/jelly
500 ml/2 cups milk, chilled
4 scoops vanilla ice cream
1 teaspoon vanilla extract
6 mini doughnuts, to serve

2 soda glasses, chilled
wooden skewers

SERVES 2

Using a clean pastry brush, brush stripes of strawberry jam/jelly onto the inside edges of the two glasses to decorate.

Thread 3 mini doughnuts onto each skewer and set aside until needed.

Put the remaining two tablespoons of jam/jelly into a blender with the milk, 2 scoops of ice cream and the vanilla extract, and whizz until foamy and thick. Pass through a sieve/strainer to remove the strawberry seeds.

Return the milkshake to the blender and blitz again to make the milkshake foamy. Pour into the prepared glasses, top each glass with a second scoop of ice cream and serve immediately with the doughnut skewers .

Cookies and cream – the popular ice cream flavour – is the inspiration for this indulgent shake. Packed full of Oreo cookies and served with extra cookies on the side, it is naughty but oh, so nice.

COOKIES AND CREAM

4 scoops cookies and cream
  or vanilla ice cream
400 ml/1⅔ cups milk
2 tablespoons Chocolate Syrup
  (see page 8 or store-bought)
8 Oreo cookies, plus extra
  to serve
canned whipped cream

2 soda glasses, chilled

SERVES 2

Put 2 scoops of the ice cream in a blender with the milk, chocolate syrup and 7 of the Oreo cookies and whizz until foamy and thick.

Pour into the chilled glasses and top each with a further scoop of ice cream. Squirt a small amount of cream on top of each milkshake.

Crush the remaining Oreo cookie and sprinkle over the milkshakes. Serve immediately with more Oreos on the side.

Raspberry Ripple – vanilla ice cream with raspberry sauce running through it – is a favourite children's dessert. Combined with raspberry or cherry soda this is the prettiest of drinks – bright pink and decorated with sugar sprinkles. Serve with a spoon for eating the fresh raspberries.

RASPBERRY RIPPLE FLOAT

4 scoops raspberry ripple ice cream
10 fresh raspberries
500 ml/2 cups raspberry or cherry soda, chilled
pink sprinkles, to decorate

2 soda glasses, chilled
2 straws

SERVES 2

Put one scoop of ice cream in the bottom of each glass and divide the raspberries between them. Top up the glasses with raspberry or cherry soda and finish with a second scoop of ice cream. Decorate with sprinkles and serve immediately with straws.

Maple syrup, candied nuts and popcorn – could you ask for anything more in a shake? If you're having a 4th July or cheerleading party, why not thread the popcorn onto foil sparkler wands to add a bit of razzle dazzle to your shakes?

MAPLE POPCORN SHAKE

40 g/1½ oz. caramel-coated
   popcorn (such as Butterkist)
4 scoops praline and cream
   ice cream
2 tablespoons maple syrup
400 ml/1⅔ cups milk, chilled

2 thin wooden skewers
2 soda glasses, chilled
2 straws

SERVES 2

Thread about 5 popcorn kernels onto each of the skewers and set aside until you are ready to serve. Take care when threading as the popcorn is fragile.

Put the ice cream, maple syrup, milk and the remaining popcorn in a blender and blitz until very foamy and thick.

Pour into chilled glasses and serve immediately with straws and the popcorn skewers.

INDULGENT

Every year I find a delicious Terry's Chocolate Orange in my Christmas stocking. Quite frankly it wouldn't be Christmas without one! This smoothie, made with orange yogurt and dark orange chocolate, is a must for all Terry's fans.

CHOCOLATE ORANGE SMOOTHIE

FOR THE CHOCOLATE ORANGE SAUCE
50 g/1½ oz. dark orange chocolate, chopped
60 ml/¼ cup golden/light corn syrup

FOR THE SMOOTHIE
300 g/1¼ cups orange yogurt
300 ml/1¼ cups milk, chilled
10 ice cubes
10 g/½ oz. milk chocolate, finely sliced, to decorate
1 tablespoon candied orange peel, to decorate (optional)

2 soda glasses, chilled
2 straws

SERVES 2

For the chocolate orange sauce, put the chopped chocolate, syrup and 1 tablespoon water in a small saucepan set over a gentle heat. Stirring all the time, heat until the chocolate has melted and you have a smooth sauce. Set aside to cool.

To prepare the smoothie, blitz the orange yogurt, milk, cooled chocolate orange sauce and ice cubes in a blender until smooth and thick. If your blender is not strong enough to crush ice, place the ice cubes in a plastic bag, seal and wrap in a clean dish towel, and bash the bag with a wooden rolling pin until the ice is crushed. Add to the blender with the other ingredients and blitz to combine.

Pour the smoothie into chilled glasses, sprinkle with chocolate slivers and orange peel, if using, and serve immediately with straws.

These milkshakes look as pretty as a picture in pastel hues of pink and lilac. The rose shake is served with shredded rose petals on top and has a fragrant floral taste, while the calming and sleep-inducing properties of lavender make this milkshake the perfect drink before bedtime. It is important to use rose petals and lavender that have not been sprayed with any chemicals.

ROSE PETAL AND LAVENDER DREAM

FOR THE ROSE PETAL DREAM
400 ml/1⅔ cups milk, chilled
4 scoops rose ice cream (such as Kulfi) or vanilla ice cream
1–2 tablespoons rose syrup, to taste
3–4 fresh rose petals, thinly shredded, to decorate
rose Turkish delight, to serve

FOR THE LAVENDER DREAM
2 teaspoons culinary lavender
50 g/¼ cup caster/granulated sugar
4 scoops vanilla ice cream
400 ml/1⅔ cups milk, chilled
a few drops of purple food colouring (optional)

4 small glasses, chilled

EACH RECIPE SERVES 4

For the **Rose Petal Dream**, put the milk and ice cream in a blender and blitz until frothy. Add the rose syrup to taste and blitz again. If you are using vanilla ice cream, add an extra spoonful of rose syrup for more rose flavour. Pour into chilled glasses and top with the shredded rose petals. Serve immediately with Turkish delight, if using.

For the **Lavender Dream** (pictured on page 1), put the lavender, sugar and 80 ml/⅓ cup water in a saucepan and simmer until the sugar has dissolved. Bring to the boil for a few minutes to form a thin syrup then remove from the heat and leave to cool. When cooled, pass the syrup through a sieve/strainer to remove the lavender buds. Put the ice cream, cooled lavender syrup and milk in a blender with a few drops of purple food colouring, if using, and blitz until smooth and frothy. Pour into chilled glasses and serve immediately.

Chocolate and cherry are an indulgent combination and this delicious drink is no exception. Thick chocolate syrup and frozen cherry yogurt are topped up with fresh cherry juice, which is available in most supermarkets and health food stores. This version is decorated with a whole cherry or, for a special treat, you could use a classic cerisette (chocolate-coated cherries with kirsch).

CHOCOLATE CHERRY FREEZE

2 tablespoons Chocolate Syrup
   (see page 8, or store-bought)
250 ml/1 cup cherry juice
2 scoops cherry frozen yogurt
canned whipped cream
chocolate sprinkles, to decorate
2 whole cherries, to decorate

2 tall, stemmed glasses, chilled

SERVES 2

Spoon a tablespoon of chocolate syrup into each glass and swirl so that the bottom third of the glass is coated with syrup.

Put the cherry juice and frozen yogurt in a blender and blitz until frothy.

Pour into the prepared glasses and top each with a squirt of whipped cream. Decorate the glasses with chocolate sprinkles and a whole cherry and serve immediately.

This milkshake is the ultimate pick-me-up – strong coffee and sweet ice cream. Coffee ice cream can sometimes be difficult to find so if it is not available you can replace it with vanilla ice cream and add another shot of espresso instead.

COFFEE FRAPPE

2 shots of espresso, cooled
350 ml/1½ cups milk
4 scoops coffee ice cream
15 ice cubes
canned whipped cream
unsweetened cocoa powder,
    for dusting
2 chocolate-coated coffee beans
    or chocolate coffee-bean
    shaped chocolates, to decorate

2 soda glasses, chilled
2 straws

SERVES 2

Put the espresso, milk and 2 scoops of coffee ice cream in a blender with the ice cubes and blitz until thick and creamy. If your blender is not strong enough to crush ice, place the ice cubes in a plastic bag, seal and wrap in a clean dish towel, and bash the bag with a wooden rolling pin until the ice is crushed, then add to the blender with the other ingredients and blitz together.

Pour the milkshake into the chilled glasses and top each glass with a scoop of coffee ice cream. Squirt a little of the cream on top of the shake, dust with cocoa and top with a chocolate coffee bean. Serve immediately with straws.

Adding a pinch of salt to a sticky caramel sauce gives a whole new depth of flavour. Topped with pieces of fudge and packed full of toffee ice cream, this shake is a creamy, caramel dream!

SALTED CARAMEL SHAKE

FOR THE SALTED CARAMEL SAUCE
100 g/½ cup caster/granulated sugar
50 g/3 tablespoons butter
a pinch of salt
3 tablespoons double/heavy cream

FOR THE MILKSHAKE
400 ml/1⅔ cups milk, chilled
4 scoops toffee/caramel ice cream
2 pieces vanilla fudge, cut into small cubes, to decorate

2 soda glasses, chilled

SERVES 2

To prepare the salted caramel sauce, put the sugar and butter in a small saucepan and simmer over a gentle heat until the butter has melted and the sugar dissolved. Add the salt and cream and heat for a further few minutes, stirring, until you have a thick sauce. Set aside to cool.

When cooled, spoon a tablespoonful of the caramel sauce into each glass and swirl so that the bottom half of the glass is coated in caramel.

Put the milk into a blender with the remaining caramel sauce (reserving a little for decoration) and two scoops of the ice cream, and blitz until smooth and frothy.

Pour the shake into chilled glasses and top each with a scoop of ice cream. Sprinkle with the fudge pieces, drizzle with the reserved caramel sauce and serve immediately.

At a summer dinner party, why not end the meal with a mint chocolate milkshake? If you want to make more of an impact, you can intensify the green with a little food colouring. Either way, these milkshakes are the perfect refreshment.

MINT CHOCOLATE MILKSHAKE

FOR THE CHOCOLATE MINT SAUCE
50 g/1½ oz. chocolate peppermint
   squares (such as After Eights)
2 tablespoons double/heavy
   cream
1 tablespoon golden/light
   corn syrup

FOR THE MILKSHAKE
4 scoops mint choc chip
   ice cream
350 ml/1½ cups milk, chilled
a few drops of green food
   colouring (optional)
chocolate sprinkles, to decorate
4 chocolate peppermint sticks
   or squares, to serve (optional)

2 soda glasses, chilled
a squeezy bottle or piping bag
   with a small round nozzle/tip

SERVES 2

To prepare the chocolate mint sauce, put the chocolate peppermint squares in a saucepan with the cream and syrup and simmer over a gentle heat, stirring, until the chocolate has melted and you have a smooth sauce. Set aside to cool.

Put the chocolate mint sauce in a squeezy bottle or piping bag and drizzle pretty patterns of sauce up the inside of each glass.

Put two scoops of the ice cream in a blender with the milk and the food colouring, if using, and blitz until smooth and frothy.

Pour into the prepared glasses, top each with a scoop of ice cream and decorate with chocolate sprinkles. Serve immediately with more chocolate peppermint squares or chocolate peppermint sticks, if using.

When I was writing this book, my friend Julia told me of a delicious pistachio milkshake that she was served in a Greek island harbour while waiting for a ferry. Of course, I had to recreate it straight away. This is a truly exotic milkshake – perfect for hot days when you would rather be on a beach in Greece! Pistachio syrup is available from online shops and is a pretty way to decorate your milkshake glasses.

PISTACHIO SHAKE

6 scoops pistachio ice cream
400 ml/1⅔ cups milk, chilled
pistachio syrup, to decorate
   (optional)

2 soda glasses, chilled
2 straws

SERVES 2

Put the ice cream in a blender with the milk and blitz until foamy and thick.

Decorate the glasses with a swirl of pistachio syrup, if using, then pour in the milkshake and serve immediately with straws.

INDEX